Science Experiments
WITH
WATER

Sally Nankivell-Aston
and Dorothy Jackson

W
FRANKLIN WATTS
A Division of Grolier Publishing
NEW YORK • LONDON • HONG KONG • SYDNEY
DANBURY, CONNECTICUT

Picture credits: The Stock Market 4 (tl, bl, bm), 15 (br); Images Colour Library 4 (tr), 11 (bm), 14 (bl), 23 (br); Oxford Scientific Films 4 (br Duncan Murrell), 6 (bl Daniel Valla), 9 (tr Heikki Nikki), 17 (tr London Scientific films), 21 (tr Richard Packwood), 24 (bl Richard Packwood), 28 (br John Downer); Ecoscene 27 (t Sally Morgan).

Thanks, too, to our models: Kreena Davy, Aaron Gupta, George Marney, Charlotte Sipi, Ahmani Vidal-Simon and David Watts.

Editor: Claire Berridge
Art director: Jonathan Hair
Picture research: Sue Mennell
Photography: Ray Moller
(unless otherwise credited)
Artwork: Peter Bull (pp 5 and 19)
Cover photography: Steve Shott

First published in 1999 by Franklin Watts

First American edition 2000 by Franklin Watts/Children's Press
A Division of Grolier Publishing
90 Sherman Turnpike
Danbury
CT 06816

ISBN 0-531-14575-1 (hbk)
      0-531-15432-7 (pbk)

Catalogue information available from the Library of Congress.

GROLIER
PUBLISHING

Visit Franklin Watts/Children's Press on the Internet at:
http://publishing.grolier.com

Contents

Water Everywhere

W ATER COVERS ABOUT THREE-QUARTERS of the Earth's surface. It is essential to all life on Earth. Plants and animals need water to survive — and that includes us!

Water can be hot, cold, or warm. It can be loud or quiet.

Water can be found in three different forms — solid, liquid, or gas.

Be Amazed

By doing the experiments in this book you can find out some amazing things about water. You will find out about how it changes, mixes, separates, and pushes things along. Some experiments may answer questions that you already ask about water. Some may make you think of more!

Look Closely

Scientists always ask lots of questions and observe carefully. When you are doing the experiments in this book, look closely to see what is happening. Remember to make sure you keep accurate records of all your results — like all good scientists!

Be Careful

Always make sure an adult knows that you are doing an experiment, and ask for help if you need to cut or heat something, use hot water, glass, or anything else that could be dangerous. Follow the step-by-step instructions carefully and remember — be a safe scientist!

Can you spot six ways water is being used in this picture?

Water on the Move

I**N ITS LIQUID FORM,** water can flow through pipes and will fill different shaped containers. It can be made to travel downward and upward and even to squirt high into the air! Do the following experiment to find out how.

✓ You will need
- ✓ a large funnel
- ✓ a long piece of tubing
- ✓ insulating tape
- ✓ a large jug
- ✓ transparent outer case of a ball point pen
- ✓ water

In Action

Water is stored in reservoirs or water towers. If the reservoir or tower is higher than the houses it is supplying, the water pressing down pushes the water through the pipes to our homes. If the reservoir or tower is lower, then the water needs to be pushed through with a pump.

1 Tape the funnel to one end of the tubing using the insulating tape.

2 In the same way, tape the wider end of the pen case to the other end of the tubing.

3 Holding the pen upright and just above the level of the funnel, ask a friend to carefully pour the water into the funnel until it fills the tubing and about half of the funnel.

4 Hold the pen still, then slowly lift the funnel upward. Look closely to see what happens.

5 Lift the funnel a bit higher. As you do this, the water presses down more so that it pushes harder through the tube. What happens to the water in the tube now, and why do you think this happens?

Keep Thinking

You can stop the flow of water in a pipe by turning off the tap. This closes the end of the pipe. What would happen if you put your finger over the end of the pen case in the experiment, then took your finger away?

Don't Stop There

● Fill a variety of different shaped containers with water and watch the way the water takes on the shape of each container. What happens to the water's surface if you tilt one of the containers? Does it tilt with the container or does it remain horizontal?

Cold as Ice!

WHEN WATER GETS very cold, it changes from a liquid to a solid, which is called "ice." This process is called freezing. Water freezes at 32°F (0°C) — this is its freezing point. In this experiment we will find out more about what happens when water turns to ice.

1 Carefully put the opening of your balloon over a tap. Turn the tap on and slowly fill the balloon about 3/4 full with water. Tie it up.

2 Measure the distance around the balloon at its widest point (mark the position with the pen) and keep a record of this measurement.

3 Put the balloon in a freezer for a few hours or overnight.

4 Take it out and look closely to see what has happened.

In Action

When the weather is really cold, you can see the effects of water freezing. Snow, hail, frost, and ice are various forms of frozen water. Some parts of the world are so cold that ice sheets cover land and sea and there are icebergs in the water.

5 Measure the balloon again along the line you made with the pen.

6 Has the balloon gotten bigger or smaller? What do you think has happened to the water inside the balloon as it changed from a liquid to a solid? Has it changed in other ways?

7 Try floating your ice balloon in a large bowl of water. It will float like a giant ice cube because it is less dense than water — it is lighter for its size.

Don't Stop There

• Take six ice cubes. Put each one on a saucer in different places around the house. Look at your cubes every 10 minutes. It's a race to see which one melts the fastest! Think about why ice melts. What makes the winner melt first?

• You can put things on ice to make it melt more quickly. Take two ice cubes. Leave one as it is and pour salt on the other. Compare the time they take to melt. Why do you think salt is put on icy roads?

Vanishing Water?

WHERE DO YOU THINK water goes when puddles dry up, clothes dry on the line, ponds dry up, and spilled water seems to disappear? Do you ever wonder where the rain comes from, and why the windows sometimes get damp and misty? Try this simple experiment to find out more.

✓ **You will need**

- ✓ a transparent bowl
- ✓ modeling clay
- ✓ jug of hot water from the tap
- ✓ clear plastic wrap

1 Make the banks of a lake with the modeling clay, about a third of the way up the sides of the transparent bowl. Add small toy models of animals, trees, and houses to create a scene.

2 Fill the lake with hot water. Ask an adult to help.

3 Quickly stretch the plastic wrap over the top of the bowl and seal it along the edge by pressing it firmly.

4 Watch as water droplets appear on the inside of the bowl and the plastic wrap. Where does this water come from? Can you see the droplets of water on the wrap fall like rain and run down the sides of the bowl?

The Water Cycle

Water on the Earth's surface (such as in lakes, rivers, and the sea) evaporates into the atmosphere as water vapor when it is heated up by the Sun. You cannot see it, but it rises high up, cools and condenses (turns back into liquid), and forms clouds. Water from the clouds eventually falls down to Earth again as rain.

In Action

When you see dew in the morning, it is water vapor from the air that has condensed during the evening or in the night, if it gets cooler.

Don't Stop There

● On a sunny day, make a puddle by pouring water onto some hard ground. Draw around the puddle with chalk. Return to the puddle regularly and draw around it each time. How does the shape of the puddle change? Does all the water evaporate or could some of it be soaking into the ground? How long does it take to dry up?

Boiling Hot!

WHEN WATER GETS very hot, it boils and changes from a liquid into a gas, which is hot water vapor. This vapor is sometimes called steam. Find out more about what happens when water boils.

SAFETY. An adult must help you with this experiment.

✓ You will need

- ✓ homemade tongs
  (wooden clothes peg stuck securely onto
  a 1 1/2-foot [1/2 meter] length of thin wood)
- ✓ baking tray
- ✓ aluminum foil container
- ✓ candle
- ✓ matches
- ✓ sand
- ✓ water

1 Cover the bottom of the baking tray with a layer of sand about 1 in. (3 cm) deep.

2 Put a candle in the center of the tray and ask an adult to help you light it.

3 Attach the aluminum foil container to the peg on the tongs. Put a small amount of water inside.

4 Hold the aluminum foil container over the candle flame using your homemade tongs. Watch to see what happens, but do not lean over the candle to look at the water. Instead, occasionally bring the container toward you and look inside, away from the flame.

5 What is happening to the water? Can you see anything coming off it? What do you think it is? Does it smell, or have a color?

Keep Thinking

Have you ever noticed that windows in a kitchen sometimes "steam up" when water is boiling on a stove or in a kettle? Why is this happening? Look back at pages 10-11 for a clue.

6 Continue heating until all the water has boiled away. Where has it gone? Can you see steam now? Where does the steam go?

Don't Stop There

● How long does water take to boil? Ask an adult to help you with this. Predict how long it takes to boil 3 cups of water from tap temperature to boiling. Put 3 cups of tap water into an empty kettle. Then time how long it takes for the kettle to boil. Was your prediction correct? Try boiling 2 and then 4 cups of water. Which takes longer to boil?

● Water boils at 212°F (100°C). We call this its boiling point. Sometimes you may say you feel "boiling hot." Are you really? Using a thermometer, find out your body temperature (in °F).

Rainy Days

When we have wet weather, water falls to the ground as rain. Sometimes rain falls in light showers; other times it comes in heavy storms. Find out how much rain falls where you live or go to school.

In Action

Water does not always fall as rain. If the weather is very cold, the water falls as forms of ice: hail, sleet, or snow. Sometimes mist or fog forms. Fog and mist are really clouds at ground level. They form when water vapor in the air comes in contact with cold ground. It condenses into water droplets. Thick fog can be very dangerous because it is difficult to see through.

✓ **You will need**
- 6 large plastic soda bottles
- scissors
- plastic ruler

1 Ask an adult to help you cut the top off each bottle, approximately two-thirds from the bottom.

2 Turn the tops over and put them back onto the bottles. The tops will act as funnels. You have now made your own rain collectors.

3 Put the bottles in different places outside — in the open, under trees, beside the house.

DAY	BOTTLE 1	BOTTLE 2	BOTTLE 3	BOTTLE 4	BOTTLE 5	BOTTLE 6
MON.						
TUES.						
WED.						
THURS.						
FRI.						
SAT.						
SUN.						
MON.						
TUES.						
WED.						
THURS.						
FRI.						
SAT.						
SUN.						

4 Each day at the same time, measure how much rain has collected in each bottle. Do this every day for two weeks, and record the amounts in a table like this. Remember to throw the water away after you measure each day!

5 Look at your table. On which day did the most rain fall? On which day did the least rain fall? Which bottle collected the most rain over the two weeks? Why do you think that happened? Which collected the least? Why?

Don't Stop There

● Repeat the experiment, but this time record how much cloud cover there is on each day as well. To do this, put a large mirror on the ground and estimate how much of it is covered by clouds. Are the cloudiest days the wettest?

● What type of clouds lead to rain? Next time it rains, see what the rain clouds look like.

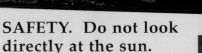

SAFETY. Do not look directly at the sun.

Water's Skin

HAVE YOU EVER LOOKED closely at the surface of a very full glass of water? The surface of the water is above the top of the glass! It's as if there is a skin on the water — it will even hold a small paper clip! Try this experiment to find out more about water's mysterious skin.

✓ You will need
- ✓ tray of water
- ✓ dishwashing liquid
- ✓ thin cardboard or plastic
- ✓ drinking straw or dropper

1 Make a little fish shape about 3 inches (8 cm) long out of the plastic or cardboard.

2 Cut a funnel shape out of the tail.

3 Place the fish on the surface of the water at one end of the tray.

In Action

There are some tiny creatures called water striders (right) that can use the surface tension to walk on water. There is also a species of lizard called the Basilisk lizard that can run across the water surface without sinking.

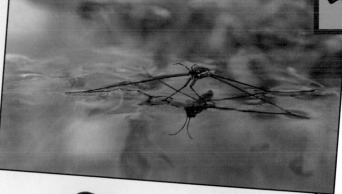

4 Fill the dropper or straw with a little dishwashing liquid. Very carefully put one drop onto the "funnel" in the fish and watch. What do you think is happening? How does it work?

Surface Tension

The tiny particles of water are held together like a weak net, which forms a stretchy invisible skin around the water. This effect is called surface tension. The net can be broken by detergents.

Don't Stop There

● Do you think other soapy liquids will behave in the same way? Try the experiment again using liquid soap. (Remember to clean the tray out first!) What happens to the fish? Does it move as fast?

● Spray a little colored water from a plant mister onto a clean smooth surface and look closely at the drops of water. What shape are they? Can you think why?

Message in a Bottle

IN STORIES, SHIPWRECKED people sometimes put a message in a bottle and throw it into the sea. They hope that it will float and be found by someone who will rescue them. Do this experiment to find out if this idea will work.

✓ **You will need**
✓ paper and pencils for writing messages
✓ a selection of glass and plastic bottles with lids
✓ a water tank, sink, or bath
✓ water

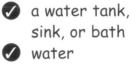

1 Pretend that you are stranded on a desert island. Write some rescue messages and put one in each of the bottles.

2 Put the lids on and predict which will float and which will sink.

3 Now test to see if your predictions are correct by putting the bottles carefully into the water. Shake the water a bit so it is like the real sea! Which bottles float and which sink? What is inside the floating bottles that helps them stay afloat?

4 Now take the bottles out of the sink and remove the lids. Predict which ones will float now. To make the test fair, put them in and shake the "sea" in the same way as before.

Keep Thinking

Lifejackets and water wings use air to make them float. Can you think of any other examples of objects that float because they have air inside?

5 Which bottles float now? Was this what you predicted? Why do you think this happened? What has gone in to the bottles and what has come out? Which of your bottles would be the best for sending a message? Would you put the lid on? Why or why not?

In Action

Some fish have swim bladders inside them. Air can enter this bladder. This allows the fish to control its depth in the water. Without the swim bladder most fish would sink to the bottom.

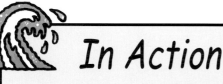

Swim bladder

Don't Stop There

● Do artificial and natural sponges float? Put one of each in water. Squeeze them both until you get as much air out of the holes as you can. Look closely to see what happens when you let go.

SOMETIMES SEAWATER is polluted when oil is accidentally spilled by oil tankers. This can have a devastating effect on wildlife. Find out what happens when oil is added to water in this next experiment.

✓ You will need
- ✓ a transparent bowl
- ✓ water
- ✓ sand
- ✓ cooking oil
- ✓ stones and shells
- ✓ dishwashing liquid
- ✓ model boat

1 Make a model of a rock pool using the bowl, stones, shells, sand, and water. Float a boat on your pool.

2 Pour some cooking oil into your rock pool to make it look like an oil slick. Look closely to see what happens. Does the oil float or sink?

3 Mix the oil and water together. Look closely to see what happens. Does it mix up? Does it stay mixed or does it separate?

In Action

If oil is spilled into the sea (like in this picture) it can cause damage to the environment. Birds can get covered with it. Detergents like dishwashing liquid are used to help remove the oil from the feathers.

4 Now add some dishwashing liquid and stir it up with the oil and water. What happens? Has this made them mix better or is one still on top?

5 Whether a liquid floats or sinks depends on how dense it is. A less dense liquid will float on a more dense one. What does this tell you about oil and water?

Don't Stop There

● Do you think molasses will float on top of water? Take a glass of water. Carefully pour a tablespoon of molasses into the glass. Does it float or sink?

● Make your own colorful drink! Take a tall glass and pour in water until it is about 3/4 full. Now carefully add a tablespoon of orange juice, then a tablespoon of a different colored juice drink. Look closely to see what happens to the liquids. Drink from each layer with a straw. Can you taste the different flavors?

Mix It Up

WHEN SOMETHING MIXES completely with water, it has dissolved. Many things can dissolve in water — not only solid things like powders, but also liquids and gases. Some things will not mix with water at all (look back at pages 20–21). Some things partly dissolve in water. Try this experiment with a friend to help solve the problem of the jars of kitchen ingredients that have lost their labels, and to see which solids mix or dissolve in water.

✓ **You will need**
✓ very fine granulated sugar
✓ salt
✓ cornstarch
✓ bicarbonate of soda
✓ 8 small plastic cups
✓ marker pen and labels
✓ 4 spoons
✓ cold water in a jug

1 Put two teaspoons of each different powder in its own separate cup. Label the cups 1, 2, 3, and 4. Keep a secret record of which letter matches each powder.

2 Tell your friend you have sugar, salt, cornstarch, and bicarbonate of soda but need their detective skills to find out which is which. Give them the clues (in the box below) to help identify the powders.

SUGAR — dissolves (mixes completely) in cold and warm water.
SALT — partly dissolves in cold water; dissolves in warm water.
CORNSTARCH — partly dissolves in cold water and makes a cloudy liquid. May get lumpy in warm water.
BICARBONATE of SODA — partly dissolves in cold and warm water; fizzes slightly.

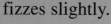

3 Pour a little COLD water into cup 1. Mix it up with a spoon. Count the number of stirs. Look closely to see what happens. Does the powder mix completely (dissolve) with the water? Does it partly mix, not mix at all, or do anything else? Get your friend to take notes.

4 Repeat step 3 for cups 2, 3, and 4. Make sure you stir the powders the same number of times as before.

5 With fresh cups of powder, repeat the test using WARM water. Don't forget the detective notes of the results! Let your friend use the clues to decide which powder is which.

Don't Stop There

● Try mixing some other kitchen substances with water. You could use instant coffee, cocoa, dried milk, fruit juice, vinegar, and cooking oil. What else can you think of? What did you notice about how they mix with water?

In Action

Pollution in the atmosphere dissolves in the water in clouds — you can't see it, but it's there. This is called acid rain, which is strong enough to dissolve some types of stone. Many buildings and statues are damaged in this way.

Water Splits It Up

BESIDES BEING USED to mix substances together, water can also be used to separate out certain substances — even things you can't see! Try this experiment to find out how water can do this.

✓ You will need
- ✓ 2 eggcups
- ✓ sand
- ✓ salt
- ✓ a funnel
- ✓ thin piece of cloth
- ✓ a container
- ✓ cold water
- ✓ a shallow dish

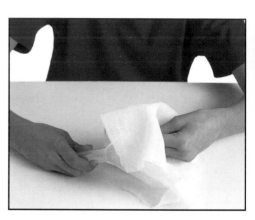

1 Mix an eggcup full of sand with an eggcup full of salt.

2 Then line the funnel with the piece of thin cloth to make a filter.

In Action

In some parts of the world, you can see the effect of water evaporation from the sea. Large beds of dried salt are left behind where there was once seawater.

3 Pour the mixture of sand and salt into the funnel.

4 Then put the funnel over a container and pour cold water into it. Look closely as the liquid pours through the funnel. What is in the liquid you see in the container? What is left in the filter?

Don't Stop There

● When you use a felt tip pen, it looks like you are writing in one color. But sometimes the color you see is really a mixture of different colors. You can use water to split them up. Take six pieces of coffee filter paper and six different colors of felt tip pen. Draw a large spot in the center of every filter paper, using a different color each time. Use a pipette and slowly drop water onto the spot. Look closely to see what happens. Try this experiment again with food colorings or ink.

5 Pour some of this liquid into a shallow dish and leave it in a warm place. After a few days what do you notice? Can you see anything in the dish? Where do you think the water has gone (look back to pages 10-11)?

6 You have already discovered that some substances dissolve in water and some don't. Which substance in this experiment dissolved in water?

Water for Life

WHAT HAVE YOU USED water for today? Think of all the ways you use water — for drinking, washing, cleaning your teeth, flushing the toilet! We use a lot of water every day, and all living things need water. They do not all need the same amount of water or get it in the same way, but all plants and animals need water for life. Try this experiment to find out more.

1 Nearly fill each cup with compost. Then draw a funny face on each one and label them A, B, and C.

2 Sprinkle a large pinch of seeds into each cup — try to put the same amount in each one.

3 Pour the same amount of water into each one — to make the compost damp. Put the cups in a light place.

In Action

Some plants and animals live in very dry places, and they have developed special ways of getting or storing water. Cactuses are a good example of plants that store water to survive in their harsh environment.

4 Keep giving the SAME amount of water for a few days until you see green shoots growing above the edges of the cups.

5 Now start to change the conditions! STOP watering A. Give B the SAME amount of water as before. FILL C to the brim every day.

Don't Stop There

● With a simple experiment you can see the tiny tubes that carry water around a plant. Put a few drops of food coloring in water in a tall container. Cut the end off a stick of celery and immediately put the stick in the water. Leave it overnight and look closely to see what has happened. What do you notice? Take the celery out of the water, and carefully cut the stem across and look at the cut end. Can you see the color now?

6 Look closely and keep a check on the cups. Is the grass growing the same way in each cup? In which one is it growing best? Can you think of reasons why? What does the grass need to grow? Turn the cups around and draw a new face on them to show how well the grass grew. What sort of face will you draw — happy or sad?

Water Power!

WATER CAN BE USED to make things move. Play this squirty competition and find out more about water power.

✅ **You will need**
- ✅ water tray (or use the bathtub!)
- ✅ 2 straws or wooden sticks and paper to make flags
- ✅ 2 table tennis balls (numbered or different colors)
- ✅ 2 squirters filled with water (eg: dishwashing liquid bottle, plant sprayer, a toy that squirts water)

1 Set up the "racing pool" with two flags as finish-line flags.

2 Half fill the tray with water.

3 Place the table tennis balls at the starting end.

In Action

The energy from moving water can be used to turn turbines for generating electricity. Hydroelectric power stations and dams use water in this way to supply electricity to whole communities.

4 Each person squirts water from their squirter to try and push their ball to the finish line! First one past the line is the winner.

5 Which was the best squirter? Why do you think the water was more powerful from this one? How did the water move to push the ball along?

Don't Stop There

● What other floating objects can you move using water in a squirter? Does the size of the object make any difference? Do you need more or less water power to move the heavier objects? Does the squirter work best when it is very full of water or nearly empty?

Glossary

This glossary gives the meaning of each word as it is used in this book.

Acid rain Rain that has pollution from the air dissolved in it.
Atmosphere The layer of air that surrounds the Earth.

Boiling point When a liquid, such as water, begins to turn into gas. The boiling point of water is 212°F (100°C).
Boil When water boils it changes into a gas.

Condense To change from a gas (eg: water vapor) to a liquid (eg: water).

Dense Closely packed together particles.
Density A measure of how packed together the particles of any thing are. Everything is made up of particles (or matter).
Desert A large area of land which gets very little rain, and is often covered in sand.
Detergent A chemical, such as dishwashing liquid, that is used to clean oily, greasy, or dirty things.

Dew Water droplets that condense from the air on things outside, during cool nights.
Dissolve To mix completely with water.

Evaporate When water changes from a liquid into water vapor.
Experiment A fair test done to find out more about something, or to answer a question. Sometimes called an investigation.

Filter A way of separating substances using material with very tiny holes in it.
Float To be supported (or suspended) in a fluid (like water). Things that are less dense than water float in it.
Fog Thick mist that is difficult to see through.
Freeze When liquid water turns into solid ice (frozen water).
Frost The frozen water drops that are seen all over things outside on very cold days, making everything look white.

Gas A gas, such as air, has no fixed shape or volume. It spreads out to fill the shape of the container that it is confined in. Often you cannot see a gas.

Hail Small pellets of frozen water.
Hydroelectric power Using the energy from moving water to make electricity.

Ice Solid water. Water freezes at 32°F (0°C).
Iceberg A huge lump of ice floating in very cold seas.
Ice crystals Very tiny pieces of frozen water.

Liquid A liquid has a definite volume but it can flow and take the shape of the container it is in.

Melt To turn from a solid such as ice, into a liquid such as water.
Mist Very small drops of water vapor in the air.

Pollution Harmful substances produced by things such as factories or cars, that sometimes mixes with the air or in water.
Predict To guess what will happen in an experiment before doing it.
Pump A machine to move or lift a liquid such as water.

Reservoir A place, like a lake, where water is stored.
Result The outcome of an experiment.

Sink To fall through the water to the bottom. Things which are denser than water sink.
Snow Clumps of ice crystals that fall from the clouds when it is very cold.
Solid Solid water is called ice. It has a definite shape.
Steam Very hot water vapor.
Surface tension The skin on water.
Swim bladder An air bag found in some fish to help them control their depth as they swim in water.

Thermometer An instrument to measure temperature.
Transparent Completely see-through.
Turbine A machine with blades that can be turned by moving water and used to make electricity.

Water cycle The natural process when water evaporates into the air, rises, cools, condenses in clouds, and falls to the ground again.
Water power The energy of moving water that can move objects, or power machines.
Water tower A tall tower which stores water.
Water vapor Water when it is a gas.

Index